SCHO
N
Nonf

MW01130629

From Pinecone to Pine Tree

by Ellen Weiss

Children's Press®
A Division of Scholastic Inc.
New York Toronto London Auckland Sydney
Mexico City New Delhi Hong Kong
Danbury, Connecticut

These content vocabulary word builders are for grades 1–2.

Subject Consultant: Emily Yates, Millennium Seed Bank Project Co-coordinator, Institute for Plant Biology and Conservation, Chicago Botanic Garden, Glencoe, Illinois

Reading Consultant: Cecilia Minden-Cupp, PhD, Early Literacy Consultant and Author, Chapel Hill, North Carolina

Photographs © 2008: Alamy Images: 21 top (Peter Arnold, Inc.), cover center inset, 4 bottom right, 15, 20 bottom (Runk/Schoenberger), 5 top left, 7 (Scottish Viewpoint); Corbis Images: 19, 20 right, 21 left Mark Karrass), cover background (Don Mason), 23 top left (David Ponton/Design Pics), 4 top, 23 top right (Paul A. Souders); Getty Images: back cover, 4 bottom left, 17, 21 right (Peter Forest), 23 bottom right (Rich Reid), cover right inset, 5 bottom right, 17 inset, 21 bottom (Steve Satushek); Masterfile/F. Lukasseck: 9; Peter Arnold Inc./Ed Reschke: 2, 5 bottom left, 13, 20 center left; Photo Researchers, NY: 23 bottom left (Gregory G. Dimijian, M.D.), cover left inset, 1, 5 top right, 11, 20 top left (Robert J. Erwin); Visuals Unlimited/Scientifica: 13 inset.

Book Design: Simonsays Design!
Book Production: The Design Lab

Library of Congress Cataloging-in-Publication Data
Weiss, Ellen, 1949–
    From pinecone to pine tree / by Ellen Weiss.
        p. cm.—(Scholastic news nonfiction readers)
    Includes bibliographical references and index.
    ISBN-13: 978-0-531-18537-7 (lib. bdg.) 978-0-531-18790-6 (pbk.)
    ISBN-10: 0-531-18537-0 (lib. bdg.) 0-531-18790-X (pbk.)
    1. Pine—Life cycles—Juvenile literature. I. Title. II. Series.
    QK494.5.P66W45 2007
    585'.2—dc22   2007010158

CONTENTS

WORD HUNT

Look for these words as you read. They will be in **bold**.

conifers
(**kah**-nuh-furz)

seedling
(**seed**-ling)

seeds
(seedz)

pinecones
(**pine**-kohnz)

pollen
(**pol**-uhn)

woody
(**woo**-dee)

shoot
(shoot)

Cones Make More Trees

Do you see the **pinecones** on this pine tree?

They are an important part of the tree.

The cones are how pine trees make more trees.

pinecones

One pine tree may have hundreds of pinecones.

Trees with cones are called **conifers**.

Conifers have **seeds**, but the seeds are not inside fruits.

Conifers are some of the oldest seed plants on Earth.

This type of plant has been around for more than 300 million years!

Bristlecone pines are the oldest type of living thing on Earth.

Pine trees have male cones and female cones.

Male pinecones are smaller than female pinecones. Male cones grow earlier in the spring.

The male cones are full of **pollen**.

Pollen is a special dust that helps plants make new seeds.

The wind blows a cloud of pollen off of this male pinecone.

Young female cones are soft and green.

Over time, they grow larger and become **woody**.

They make seeds that can grow to be new pine trees.

Female pinecones turn brown and woody as they grow.

young female pinecone

13

Pollen from male pinecones blows through the air.

Some of it lands on the female cones.

The pollen helps the female cones make seeds.

When a female pinecone opens up, the seeds fall out.

Many pine seeds are eaten by squirrels and other animals.

Wind and animals move the seeds around.

When a pine seed lands on the ground, it sends roots into the soil.

Soon a little green **shoot** pokes out of the earth.

The shoot will become a **seedling** if it gets enough sunlight and water.

shoot

A pine tree seedling grows
in a field of flowers.

A seedling with enough room to grow will become a new pine tree.

Next time you see a pinecone, take a closer look.

That brown, woody cone has an important job to do!

Taking a hike through a forest is a good way to learn more about pine trees!

PINE TREE LIFE CYCLE

1 ..... Pollen from a male pinecone lands on a female pinecone.

2 ..... The female pinecone makes seeds.

5

In a few years, the tree grows its own cones.

4

The pine seedling grows.

3

The seed starts to grow and a shoot appears above the soil.

YOUR NEW WORDS

conifers (**kah**-nuh-furz) trees that produce cones

pinecones (**pine**-kohnz) male and female parts of pine trees

pollen (**pol**-uhn) tiny yellow grains made by the male parts of plants

seedling (**seed**-ling) a young plant grown from a seed

seeds (seedz) the parts of plants that can grow into new plants

shoot (shoot) a very young plant that has just broken through the soil

woody (**woo**-dee) made of wood like the hard parts of a tree

cypress
(**sye**-prus)

fir
(fur)

giant sequoia
(**jye**-uhnt si-**kwoi**-uh)

spruce
(sproos)

INDEX

FIND OUT MORE

Book:

Mattern, Joanne. *How Pine Trees Grow*. Milwaukee, WI: Weekly Reader Early Learning Library, 2006.

Website:

Real Trees 4 Kids!
http://www.realtrees4kids.org/threefive/conifers.htm

MEET THE AUTHOR

Ellen Weiss has received many awards for her books for kids. She has a garden, where she is especially good at growing weeds.